I0187102

Whispering *in a* Mad Dog's Ear

by Rick Smith

ISBN 978-1-929878-50-5

First edition

LUMMOX Press
PO Box 5301
San Pedro, CA 90733
www.lummoxpress.com

Printed in the United States of America

This book is set in ITC Galliard

Acknowledgments:

Our thanks to the editors of the following journals and anthologies where some of these poems have previously appeared: Appearances, Ascent, Aspect, Bluestem (aka Karamu), Box 749, Burning Bush, Cadillac Cicatrix, Chaffey Review, Chowder Review, City Works, Earth's Daughters, Exit 13, Hanging Loose, Hospital Drive, InterMedia, Into The Teeth of The Wind, Invisible City, Lalitamba, Lungfull!, Main Street Rag, Malpais Review, Muse, Neuropsychiatric Poetry Consortium, Off The Coast, OnTheBus, paper plates, Paper Street, Poesy, Poetry/L.A., Poetry Motel, Pomona Valley Review, Raw Dog Post Card Series, Rhino, Riverview, Roux Magazine, Say It At My Wedding, Silver Birch Review, Statement, Stonecloud, Stray Dog, "88", Aspect Anthology (1981), a chaos of angels (Wordwalker Press, 2006), Impact (Telling Our Stories Press, 2012), Last Call (LUMMOX Press, 2011), Lost Highway (LUMMOX Press, 2000), Reeds and Rushes (Puddinghouse Press, 2010), So Luminous The Wildflowers (Tebot Bach, 2003) Together Again For The First Time (2013), Working The Wreckage of The American Poem (LUMMOX Press, 2011), vanishing point, Baby Luv (coffee house scene) (Mojave Films, 1999).

The author wishes to recognize and thank some of those who have inspired, encouraged and assisted with this work: Blaise Cendrars, Pierre Reverdy, Paul Eluard, Vicki Lindner, Llyn Foulkes, Lorine Parks, R. Kim Smith, Donald Justice, Alice Pero, Gary Brower, Michael C Ford, John (the shape maker) Lyon, Jim Carroll, Gary Winkel, Little Walter Jacobs, Shakey Tim Robertson, Michelle Dowd, Chris Hurtado, Buk, Angela Copple, Deborah Clark Yeseta, John Brantingham, Judy Bever and Chris (Wren Noir) Yeseta. My wife, Erika, deserves special acknowledgment for her feedback on early drafts. And finally, to Raindog, who jump-started my writing back in the '90s after it had stalled out and rolled into a rest-stop. Thanks to him for giving so many poets a more public voice for the past 20 years.

TABLE OF CONTENTS

Whispering
in a
Mad Dog's
Ear

Introduction

I FIRST MET RICK SMITH in person in the early '90s at Sacred Grounds in San Pedro, CA, where he was playing harmonica with the band Go Figure. I say "in person" because I had unknowingly "met" him back in the mid '70s when he co-edited a magazine called Stonecloud out of Stanford, CA. Stonecloud had some of the unique voices that would later become stalwarts of the L.A. poetry scene and Rick's handwriting was all over the walls of Stonecloud, even though I wasn't able to perceive it at the time. It was one of his many hidden talents as I would later come to find out.

Initially I knew him only as a talented songwriter and musician. But soon after I discovered that he was also a journeyman poet, who took his craft very seriously. He had the chops to back it up too, having been published in a variety of stand alone "littles" as Bukowski called them, like The Wormwood Review (a magazine I discovered after its demise and would have given my eye teeth to get into). L.A. go-to poet MC Ford once wrote about Smith "There are only a handful of poets who have located their own personal metaphor... William J. Margolis and his Australian eucalyptus tree, for Hart Crane: Brooklyn Bridge, for Bill Pillin: the ceramic wheel of the pottery maker, for Kenneth Patchen: the steel mills of Wheeling and Youngstown. And, for you, well, there's the enterprising wren."

I have always liked Rick's style of poetry. He has a wonderfully spare quality, almost as if he's writing Haiku. Gerald Locklin refers to this as the Iceberg Theory, where one doesn't need to describe a red chair any more than observing that *it* is a red chair (the idea being that we all see our own red chair anyway, so why take away from our vision of it). I believe that Rick is a master at conveying this, no matter what the red chair is: a feeling, a situation or a moment caught between worlds. The sparseness of his imagery appeals to me in a way that borders on the visceral. Perhaps it's because I lean in the direction of lonely streets and lost causes. Either way, I have never been disappointed by Rick Smith's poetry.

This is the third collection of poems by Smith published by the LUMMOX Press and a big departure from the previous two which dealt with the diminutive Wren as a metaphor for the human condition. In this volume, the gloves come off and Smith takes on the human condition, head on.

I am proud to call Rick my friend and to have him as a part of the LUMMOX family.

RD Armstrong
Publisher
LUMMOX Press

Some Little Known Facts About The Doctor

LATE ONE NIGHT about thirty years ago Rick and I were headed down the Pasadena freeway when an eighteen-wheeler that had somehow managed to get on going the wrong way suddenly appeared up ahead, coming straight at us in the fast lane. Rick somehow managed to pull over, flash his high beams, honk the horn, roll down his window and start waving to the driver, seemingly all at the same time. While my first thought had been 'great, we're going to be killed because of somebody else's mistake' Rick immediately thought of the people behind us who might not be able to react in time and acted to save everyone, not just us. He yelled to the driver, who thankfully also stopped, and pointed out the problem. As we drove away we were treated to the rare sight of a big rig trying to pull a Y-turn in the middle of an old three-lane freeway.

When he was counseling at Rancho Los Amigos he would inventory the skills that his patients still had after their traumatic injuries and identify jobs that called for those same skills, achieving a far higher placement rate than typical institutional approaches at that time. Once, while walking his dog Mabellene on a beach that had a leash law, he solved the problem posed by cops showing up across the way by miming a leash until they left. I can't count the number of times I have seen him relate to someone when no one else seemed willing or able to, and at least help get them pointed in the direction of whatever it was they wanted or needed. His ability to balance empathy with analysis is unusual and powerful.

He has always put together images and references into scenarios that seems eerily familiar, but you can't quite put your finger on why. So when he writes a poem from the point of view of a bird, or a guy who is being shot at, I am not that surprised anymore but still just as delighted every time a new batch of them turns up.

John Lyon

[attach cable to the nerves. hands
and arms wet with machine oil.
goggles must be tight. leave all
writing to the machine. words stagger
out. old women from burning buildings.]

On the Lam
(for Allen Ginsberg and Robert Johnson)

Elevated alpha readings,
trace heavy metals
and the bittersweet aftertaste
of bad water
drives the poetry watchdogs
into a lather.
They chew off their own leathers
and send us packing,
they bite at our tires
before turning away
spent and thirsty.

We have the reputation
of snake oil entrepreneurs,
back alley dilettantes
who die in dumpster fires,
rooming house fires,
if we're lucky.
We study freight schedules,
bus routes,
blue highways,
mountain trails,
we know
how to get out of town.

Even in dream,
there is a howling
upon us
in ever sharpening
Doppler pitch.

We come to you
with medicine we
come to you breathless,
we come to you
with hellhounds on our trail.

The Future

We eat cherry pie with our fingers
and lean against a 1953 Buick
gleaming in the heat.
I don't remember the other kid's name
but looking at the photographs
I know perfection
when I see it.

Writing in the dark,
embracing a false
but logical surface.
When lights go out
life goes on
and if you dip skin deep
into shadow and ink,
you only want more.

This is a blue room
and a girl sits at a yellow table.
Something like a tulip
is on the yellow table,
it seems to be on fire,
leaning over into red,
primary colors.

But it is thirst, wind
and cold that bring out
the hindbrain best
where the hand does not waver,
but stays on the page
playing out the line
beyond any edges

Poetry starts with a rope ladder
tossed into darkness
and what climbs up
lies before you, black.
It runs the border
in time-lapse frames,
holds its breath
all the way
through
the Holland Tunnel,
walks out of Safeway
with a porterhouse steak
jammed down its pants.

In my head, two telephones
are ringing and one of them
is always for me.
A voice says, "I can teach you
how to carry a grudge,
how to flourish
under the weight of luggage
without handles."

No, that's the wrong line.

I see a shooting star
and I pray for sanity.
My son pounds
fire caps on Jackson Street
in the Year of the Dog,
red on grey sidewalk.

This is the right line,
where magic turns dread
inside out.

Then there is thirst
and high wind
and sooner or later,
the rain gets to everyone.
But when I study the sky,
on the big screen,
in my near blindness,
I believe that the best
and the brightest
is still to come.

I believe men die dumb
and men die easy
in unanswerable
rain.

I believe if we live
long enough,
we will see our enemies
float by on the river,
if we live we will
eat cherry pie
with our fingers.

Rimbaud's Descent
(For Ursula K. Le Guin)

A slant of lucid madness
angles into the right hemisphere,
up the smoke filled staircase,
its metal steps booming and echoing
like they always do.
The illuminations like to dress up,
this time in polka dots
and silver ballet slippers
from Melrose Ave.
But the face, sunburned and craggy.
An old man's face, really.
Drunk and with orange lipstick
that largely
missed the lips.

Where I live begins to shake
like dice in a desperate hand.
Pictures go askew,
the piano hits a low D.
Things are amiss.
My hairbrush
crawls like a centipede
off the dresser,
across the floor.

Remove yourself
and your big hurrah,
take your bag of tricks
back to Shangri-La;
ballet dancing old man,
back to Ketchikan
where a fishing boat
rocks at your dock.

I've got my own mad shadows
speaking to me in code:
va, allez,
go live with your French speaking cousins
or push your rack down 7th Avenue.

Your flash is spectacular,
now comes the long haul.

Beating The Sea
(For Uncle Judy Lathrop)

We are at the shore
with sticks and chains.
We have come to beat the sea.
It has crawled up into our town
and taken some of our children;
we cannot allow this to be.
It has come in the afternoon
disguised as a friend
and smashed our church.
It has left our dogs
dead on the sand.

Off shore we see the sailcloth
and banners:
the cup and the torch
of southern districts.
We are standing together
ready to begin.

Dropping the Wild Horse

They say the jaw breaks even
before he hits the ground;
the crazed eyelids tear
and the jaw snaps open so wide,
the hinge cracks,
a thin thread of pain
alarms each station of the brain.
Halfway down, the legs
yield and cross crazily,
the wet nostrils pull hard
at one last pocket
of sweet milkweed

hills

(gayle's poem)

The hills north of here
roam inside the air
at the cusp of the eye.

It is the wind which gives them life.
They are musk oxen
in my red sleep.

Snow on different statues

Snow begins to fill the holes
in the quiet of the afternoon.
It settles among your chipped fingers
and indulges your porous complexion;
it lets you resemble
the rock you once were.
You have been through this before,
waiting for the Spring all night long.
Just outside your eyes
the snow drives
like insects in distress;
flakes explore your stony knees
and cover your military lap
with white chiffon.
You know the snow,
it falls on different statues
at different times
and this time is yours.
The frozen crust I step through to see you
fills in behind me
and leaves me with my own weight,
my own sound.

Landing

we've sailed through storm
and seasons
and now the harbor is before us
the sun is up
windows and roofs take shape
white sail cloth
white buildings shine
bleached and bursting
into view

it's a tourist town
where blue is grainy and soft
where white shimmers
like in the paintings they sell
in stalls by the sea
at Lahaina, Provincetown
or Laguna

all we have come through
makes our eyes squint
the sun cures us
like hide
and above us
white sail cloth
restless
brilliant
pushing us
to something firm

the destination is not the thing
it is the arriving that soaks us up
emerging detail
makes the mind go blank with promise
sheets on a line
sky and sea behind
shutters and sail cloth
slapping in a fine wind
flirting and chatty
and we forget storms
teeth-first landings
on stony shore
where force is a mood
hard as slate

for weeks
uncertainty
rules our sleep
we remember
a giddy dance
where feet
find balance
as we land
one at a time

Swans

Sure, there are swans,
silver swans, coupling swans,
swans so ominous
they remind us of something prenatal
when we were tiny and subject
to the counter-clockwise thrill
of conception and likewise
to the troubling possibilities of gravity.

Swans on Silver Lake near
where a body was found floating,
a hollow swan on our bureau,
once filled with cuff links, rings
and small change.

A pond near the house on the Cape
where one swan bedazzles herself
in early Spring
three years running.

We watch from distance,
counting the times
reflection has failed us.

Junco on the Kitchen Floor

(for Judy and Tone)

No smoke patterns
out past Camel Rock.
Just the radar gaze
of the Pojoaque Pueblo
in the Sangre de Cristo foothills.

The three of you walk
in a riverbed,
without a permit.

Coyote fencing, horse locations,
speed traps;
it's all there in the photo.

That was the day
you got a warning from the Indians.
They could have cited you,
fined you,
taken you all in
for questioning,
for being
a recognized enemy of the land,
for picking zinnias
for your little yellow table.

And, back at home,
there in the kitchen,
a junco
dead on the linoleum,
a grand presentation
from the house cat,
busy
in the wilderness.

Rafting On The Kern River *(7/07)*

ride the Kern River
in late July,
feel the broad shaft of heat
and, in shadow,
beneath an expanse of bridge
carrying trucks from Bakersfield,
the grid hums;
you can hear it
over the rush and roar.

a man my age
may fall out of a raft
at a hairpin turn
innocently named
"Deadman's Curve,"
a foot wedged against rock,
toe to toe with the stony bed,
eyes only inches from the foam of surface
and pinned by current;
he holds a final burning breath,
expects to rise,
sees light through air pockets.

sometimes a river raft
may climb onto a boulder
for no reason at noon
while a family orders shrimp scampi
at an outdoor grill in town.

ride the river as it swells
and makes its way
gargling and spitting us out
in an instant
like mouth wash.

the sound of a helicopter
takes another millennium
to arrive.

With Olivia On Mingus Mountain

You took us up to Mingus Mountain.
You said it was a spiritual place
where the eyes of the universe
look down
and bathe the land in light.

We laid out the blankets
and tied Mabellene to a rope
so she wouldn't wander off
into coyote fields.

At 3 a.m.
she barked at shadows,
took the rope to full length.
The wind went silent,
our own breath threatening to stop.

There were eyes
held fast in the flashlight beam,
four eyes,
just four
still and unblinking.
But Mabellene had four eyes of her own
so we had nothing to worry about.

I stood up,
you were calm.
You'd been here before.

When you belong to a place
there is a stillness
and what happens in the night
is behind you.
At first light
the spirit takes new shape.
And back in the city,
the asphalt heats up.

Rowing To A Place

You sit in silence
you call it prayer
or is it just listening
to your own madness
as it clears?

At a yellow table
far from the city
in a room of stucco
by a dirty river
where unmannered boats
bump together
you count your sins
until they wear you out.

You were a kid
clueless and insane
doing insane things
talking like an insane man.

Years move on,
they rush you along,
rush you to a place.
You're rowing
with your back to that place
where you now hope
never to arrive.

(after Novica Tadic)

Notes from Echo Park

The Echo Park ducks are cranky
and on edge.
When the sun goes down
some of them
sleep for only 12 seconds
at a time.
The action on shore
drives them, frantic,
into the water,
beating it senseless.

Night rhythms,
the screaming of the dispossessed,
keeps them moving,
repels them into the middle
where they can squabble
in a language
without a future tense.

photos of the lake

you speak of the lake:
the even fit of open water.
you photograph the lake,
the perfect fit.
you track
stones spinning
into the empty sky,
holding their shape,
slapping at surface.

the stones stutter
past trout and
rest with the deadwood
the moss
and the leatherbacks.
the water rises
just slightly.

you photograph the lake again.
the empty sky
the acid pan.

crisis:

The road is empty.
Near a wall
where some people have died
a radio is playing
and something's in doubt.

A man has been shooting at me.
I do not know his name.
I do not know his reason.
A man rearranges frightened air
with tiny bullets.

This is real.
I need to talk to you.

Night Sweats
(After Michael Ondaatje)

We see water
but do not see what is beneath
the tranquil surface.
We cannot see
the town it swallowed whole.

We know nothing,
the face shimmers with sweat
and fever, lips try to form words,
delirium takes over.

Now I am thinking fast
and can't breathe.
The air pockets,
I pull at them
wherever I find them.

The forehead can go cold
and I become a statue,
not thinking or moving
until the shaking starts.

If the room is dark
there is, sometimes,
one tiny glow.
A nightlight or radio
or the eye
of something closer
than it seems.

After the taxi accident

It is impossible not to notice
your hair
blows out both windows
as you pass at 60;
you are eating an orange like nothing matters.
Today is just a white day with an Italian in it
and the road crew is sweeping up glass
with big straw brooms.
The sun prepares to set.
In the mountains far away
it is too late for the farmer
who weeps beside his crop.
He has spent too much time with the earth,
he remembers about flesh.
The sun prepares to set,
the street under the lamp,
the field under moonlight,
obsessive backgrounds.
And then a woman in the northeast
walks in her front door
and finds a letter
mailed 23 years before:

you do not know me
I am waiting by the river
with a lantern and a boat

The main things aren't happening on the surface. I am still
wondering where you went that day. I was painting what I saw,
a VW with Rhode Island plates, and then everything got out of
hand. Things disappeared into line and symbol. The very physical
plates, for instance, are entirely missing. And then, the man in
the field, he knows the earth will hold him and always has. It
is twilight and at least he has a place to go. As for the mix up
with the letter. I don't know how that happened. I just don't
know how that ever happened.

Letter From Metro

A giant lizard careens out of the ruined water of Tokyo Bay and tears the roof off a power plant. It's 3 a.m. Things are never quiet at 3 a.m. It was 3 a.m. when I saw my first car wreck. But now, the tv pales in the corner and a rustling noise moves on the wall. I doze through some days and nights not far from the movie houses and magazine racks of East Hollywood. A bunch of Greeks are boating on a lake in some unlit mountain range; they are exchanging priceless gems for guns. On the North Bank of the Rio Grande, the last three Apaches weep on one another's shoulder. A man in cowboy boots leads his dog through fields of pickup trucks and ranch wagons. There are government agents out on Western Avenue, smoking and watching my window for signs. I knot the pull cord and fall back exhausted. A toilet is flushed downstairs. The drain, the action, the film, the flow, always moving. Out in Malibu, it's the same. Fish are bumping into the pier at Paradise Cove. I dream of nothing but some hard frozen river in Denmark. Everything rests. The circling police helicopter is freeze-frame. A swollen light bursts through the crackling blinds. First the light, then the dark. There is nothing to the rhythms between the blades, the channels, the wing beats, the sun cycles. We must stop asking all these stupid questions. We must stop toying with metaphysics so we can enter the beats, become the rotation. Floating with detectives in Hong Kong Harbour is not the worst thing on my mind. It is the sequels that really terrorize me. What if I don't recognize my own hands? What if I don't recognize the people or the enormous silence they're all wrapped up in? Each time I start in like this, I promise myself it's the last time. I'll write you if it happens again. I don't talk with enough people.

Old Man In Exile
(apologies to Baudelaire)

The sun sweetened your yellow hair
and before your decorated shoulders,
the people froze
in the position of prayer.
You are an old man now;
the wings of madness brush close
at your neck.

The time was April.
Flags slipped in and out of the wind
like the faces of your dictators.
You were young then,
you believed each in turn.
From within the thickness of your brocade,
questions of balance arose
like wild northern geese
and left you
light as air.

Only now do you follow yourself
down to the coast where you sit
and watch Argentina grow pale.
The cold moon is edging
across the Southern sky.
It's a revolution
you can count on.

Hector and Lulu In Phoenix

For months, Hector knew
she'd taken up with that piano teacher,
the one from the college.
The one with the long soft fingers
and the button-down shirts.
And now she's at the front door
Hector's double locked against her.
She's still working the key.
He lights two candles
with the gold Ronson
she gave him on their first anniversary,
too many years ago.

Lulu no longer needs him
for anything,
certainly not to let her in.
She won't ring the bell
but the door flies open.
She's looking at her keys,
nothing seems to fit;
he's standing before her,
grabs her arm,
pulls her in
and she tells him to fuck off.
That special stink of the piano man
is on her. Filtered cigarettes
and Stetson.

When she tries to picture Hector
lighting candles,
she just can't see it.
Maybe Hector was a little more
than she recognized,
not nearly so dumb
as she said.

But he was pretty much out of ideas,
mad with shame
and the rage
was taking him over.

It may start out
as a hairline fracture
but it moves to something
turned inside out,
something no longer able
to hold its contents.
This is the wisdom
that surfaces after 3 days
of menudo, beer
and quick shots of tequila.

When the families
go back and forth
between funeral parlors,
they light candles,
and pray
and marvel at the great job
The Hudson Bros. did
on Hector's face.

Shooting her in the heart
means that heart
will never again betray.
Shooting himself in the face
means that face
will never again shame him.

Letting Lisa find the damp bodies
means the sins of the mother
visit the daughter.

He can punish her
only once,
every time she breathes.

Votive candles in paper lunch bags
burn for Hector and Lulu.
Luminaria,
until the furious wind
crushes those tiny lights,
blows the flame right off the wick
and that's when the wide black sky
moves back into place.

The piano teacher
locks himself in the bathroom
feels his head,
holds his head with long soft fingers,
trying to keep it
from blowing off.

men afraid of only one thing

there is a man
who is afraid of nothing
that's what he tells everyone

when he stands
on a window ledge
eighteen stories up
when he chases 30 tylenol
with a tumbler of Jack
when his 3-year-old son
picks up a loaded pistol
he admits no fear
nothing scares me
he says

when the woman who
runs the household
doesn't come home
until 4 a.m.
when he's sleeping
with the mother
of his last girlfriend
when people start whispering
start disappearing with ledgers
and all their belongings
when a great aunt
is dozing
in an upstairs bedroom
with a lit cigarette
and a fogged-over mind
when dark figures are moving about
in a neighbor's garage
when he can't sleep
or keep down oatmeal
when his wife is spitting up blood,
nothing

i wake up at 3 o'clock
in the afternoon
sweating and
unable to draw breath
delirious on my deathbed
in and out of coherence
day to day
minute to minute
i see a night in july
rage drowning out
when the moon
hits your eye
over at the macaroni grill
a family unhinged
blowing about like clapboard
in high desert wind
i'm afraid only to say
i'm afraid
the rest of it is baby stuff
there are men who are afraid
of nothing

jumping off
(k jett)

she jumps off bunker tower with a full head
of coke the absolute zeroes one upon the next
push past in blurred reunion she is overwhelmed
by a cuban painting of the sea turning
into a cold sidewalk she knows she must
humor the darkness she takes a moment to
think of it she does a great sea gull
and forgets to fear the fall

Cotton Fever
(after Frank O'Hara)

Boxer floats in the Susquehanna,
one Everlast glove above the current.
He's fixed like a ram's head
in a de Chirico,
pinned inside the screen.

Silver minnows
lean into all the hollows
and where he has been
is pure liquid.

The shooting gallery night
is poised for victims of the dance
but the soul skips away,
moves with the silver.

Dawn locates the new champion.
The light will be soft,
the air still.

Rage

The demons are so near
I hear the flapping of curtains
here in the room. So near
that the thinking goes flat.
And just the blood and
its single pounding message
washes me dry. Washes
away the vision of rising
above that deadly root.

Archetypes click together,
they tumble over
like dominoes on japanese tv,
like the flapping of curtains
in my very room.
The smooth cold rock
of the heart.

Hyannis, 1982

We're in Hyannis.
It's cold.
My '65 VW
with California plates
gets me to the lot
behind the Trailways depot.
It's 11 p.m.
And January.
I got a $100 bill
from some doctor up on Liam Lane
who wants to get high.
I leave the engine running.
The lot is empty.
The 10:42 to Fall River, Pawtucket
and Providence is running late, but it's running:
taillights fading out on Rt. 6.
A guy with a Red Sox cap
under his hoodie
slips out
from the back of a building.
That's who I'm looking for.
I give him the hundred.
He hands me the coke
in a paper bindle.
I take a little taste
and pull away.
The heater hasn't worked for months
but now, I won't need it.
"One Thing Leads To Another"
comes on the radio.
I love that song.
I love this night.

You know,
Hyannis wasn't such a bad place
till the wrong kind of people
started moving in.

Renting Storage Space

We are renting storage space
outside Racine
near the lighthouse at Wind Point.
The storage space is where we hide
the things we're not supposed to have,
things they might take away
if they knew where we kept them.

(The cerebellum allows us
to go through motions
we've known since childhood)

In summer
we drive out to Wind Point,
sit by the lighthouse,
feel the breeze off Lake Michigan
and no one questions our location.
We sit in the car,
all the windows wide,
and come to terms with the heat
and with the contents
of our storage space.

If the Virgin Mary sits still
long enough on our dashboard,
we can come to terms
with the cage we've built
and with the night moths
that come and go at will
and that, sometimes, compel
us to slap our own face.

Tonight planets line up
in the western sky.
The moon peeks above the horizon,
Venus, Jupiter and Mars
stack like atlas points
of fractured extremities,
bright stitchings
overhead.

The District Attorney
has a hard-on for me
because
I live "like a prince,"
working part time,
ponying contraband
through rural crossings,
remote and anonymous,
Emo, Rainy River, Fort Frances,
International Falls.
Because
while he burns midnight oil,
I bathe in moonlight,
gaze at starlight.

These planets will not
line up like this again
until 2040 and yet
we lay low, rent storage space,
sign false documents,
cover tracks,
look over our shoulder
and, finally, fix
on the wide and trusting eyes
of our sons and daughters
who, by the minute,
get better and better
at putting two and two together.
They know
whether we've come to terms
or just gone through motions.

Next week
we'll plant liquid amber
and flowering plum trees
that can survive on this desert.

Landscape can change.
Everything can change.

I promise.

Trembling with my Angel

Those first lines,
fatter than they have to be,
burn sweet and leave that good taste
in the back of the throat.
The tongue can reach back
to taste the fever of the brain,
the sweet delirium
that makes this world softer.
The razor and the glass,
the crucifix, the altar.
And the hours roar,
the days roll,
night to day to night
and day again
and night.
We have ferocious energy.
We don't eat, we don't bathe,
we call in sick,
we miss trains, boats,
heartbeats.
By dawn of the 4th day
we are in the time
of the black bus,
bleary, trembling, sweaty,
late.
We've been talking in circles,
picking at ourselves for days.
We're scraping the glass,
still lining it up
until the nose is too swollen
to draw oxygen or powder.
We breathe through lips so dry,
the heart rumbles,
rattles the ribs,
like a monkey in a lab cage,

frantic and out of time.
When I finally close my eyes,
there's a fucking parade in my head.
Teeth are grinding like a drill team.
Then comes the dream-time:
red clay, brass out of tune
blue gum trees, crazy noise,
the laying on of clouds,
the clicking and crawling
of invisible creatures
too many to count, too tiny
to repel.
The tip of a juniper branch,
dipped in hen's blood,
plunges into my right eye.
I never fall asleep easily,
a few valiums
another beer.
I wander the outskirts
of sleep in a dawn
that reaches back
through dream fragments,
phones ringing, strobe lights,
shards of sensory interruption,
soft shapes with sharp edges.

My angel
is in the next room.
She stays at it for a couple more hours,
then lies down by me
in her panty hose.

I'm not asleep.
I'm thinking
about my mother on her death bed

with her memories
and her Vernors Ginger Ale.
It's all she could keep down.
Those last two months,
her hair dry,
like tumbleweed.
She stopped talking,
her face blank.
She stopped trying.
These images are planted behind my eye
as I fall into sleep,
into something rootless and shapeless.

A black bus backs down my alley,
motor rumbling
like a heart attack.
It's the running out
that brings me face to face
with my own shame,
my own stink.

Then,
sleep for 15 hours.
The dreams are wagons burning.

When I wake,
there are involuntary sounds
like when you're being stabbed.
Dreams are the parts
that aren't real.
But then there's
the smoke in my
apartment, the sirens
on my street.

And the hunger.
I would kill for a plate of eggs
and a cold Corona.
My hands are trembling in air,
How much money is gone this time,
how many days and nights?

I'm pouring medicine
into my ruined nostrils.
There is a soothing dampness
but not much else.
I'm promising
to stop destroying myself,
to start paying my bills.
My hands are hummingbirds,
hovering in spasm
225 times a second.
I'm counting.
And pouring coffee
in fugue time.
I'm breathing, I'm vertical,
against the odds.
But something is reminding me
death is in the neighborhood.
My angel tells me
my ride is almost here.
A black bus turns up the street.

A big soft nightmare
has a foot on my head.

Yes, I have an enemy,
my angel talks so sweet to me
but she just won't go away.
She tells me, "go get a gun."

In the early sun
I sit against a stucco wall,
spent and out of dope,
my mind in free fall,
my face sliding off my cheekbones.
All the money is gone
but it's Sunday
so I'll make work tomorrow
unless I get hold of something.

Last night, bad dream
very bad dream,
lots of red,
blood flowing through the gate
splashing up against
the lip of angel's glass
that held something red
last night.

I get greedy,
beg for a miracle.

Oh, last night, yes,
the wrong person knocked on the door
and we had to flush $300 worth of shit
down the toilet.
Then I had to drive to Silver Lake
to find a Smith & Wesson,
By 2:30 a.m. I was crouched at the window sill
watching the night for falling leaves.
I spotted a guy
in a Chinese hat
on the roof across the street.
I watched him for an hour.
Just one move and I'll blow you away.
Miraculously, the guy never does move
and weeks later he is still there.

Now I'm with my angel all the time.
She whispers she'll never leave my side.
She will protect me always.
She lies on the bed,
takes off her panty hose,
lights a cigarette
and saves the rest for me.

But if she leaves,
this tomb of a room
even for a moment,
a vulture is standing on my chest
saying Grace.

Under a well worn moon
a black bus at the curb,
the motor running.

Tattoo Highway

You always had the speed.
Speed was never the problem.
It was the lies,
your insistence on the future tense
and those betrayals by casual affiliations.
Did that actually surprise you?

You: parched relic of a soul.
Sprinting and cutting through alleys
and backstreets,
blue line crossings in frozen border towns,
fueled by rage, self-loathing, greed.
Up all night driving and waiting,
always driving and waiting...
toll booths, gas stations,
warehouses, forsaken stretches
of the Tattoo Highway.
The neon and fluorescent,
blinking and seizure inducing.
The flashlight, the match,
then darkness.
Engine blocks in the driveway,
toilets flushing up and down the street.
Then, the endless hearings at Brooklyn Federal
till finally, the other shoe dropped:
lock-downs, dirty guards,
dirty mailroom clerks,
numbing routine.

The nights come and go
but the winter takes a toll.
It lingers past its time,
leaves you government issue bedding
and the voices in your head
to get you through.

I know it's cold in there, my friend
but don't go getting angry about it.
Things could be worse.

There's two crosses out by the Tattoo Highway,
on 6A past Braintree,
running to the Cape
where no trains run,
where no river finds a way,
where the scrub pine reigns.
Out where darkness
is a hungry dog,
where the dim crescent moon
rams the edges,
where darkness stands fast,
two crosses leaning
into the perfect black night
remind us
of a slow dance
long ago
when it looked like
forever.

To The Harmonica Players

We play harmonica because we have to. We are the bastard
sons of the blues. I was born on the very same day that Charlie
Christian died and I always want to be that close to that sound.
His bus was leaving when mine was pulling in. My grandfather
played guitar, too. But he drank too much and left my
grandma with just an old amp and a baby girl. My grandma
wouldn't talk about it. Mom says he was a good-looking man,
a Cherokee from the Upper Peninsula. That's about all she
knows except they got $14 for the amp at a yard sale.

I

(What We Do)

A player will cup the harp
in hands locked and hinged.
Breath has heat and propeller blades of pure muscle
carve the tone. The sound waves will
make temperature change,
make neon shimmer and buzz.
We explore the most primal metaphysics:

God and the Devil
in hot debate
about sin and temptation,
glory and faith.
The Lord's all in,
smart money on Job.
Devil says, "go ahead, man, lay it down,
ten-to-one
the farm boy folds."

Tonight in the jaw and the chest,
in the lips, tongue and throat
there is a beating
and some door opens
before I knock.

We stand strong and keep company with
the ghosts of Charlie Christian, Les Paul,
Django and Robert Johnson
until a muddy glow appears
over Texas
until Chicago shines
like a fool
in love.

II

(Walter Jacobs/You Better Watch Yourself)

new hope, pennsylvania, 1958
a volcanic presence
irresistible and reckless,
a wild ride on the mississippi sax
from outer space

a library in iowa city, 1968,
headlines in a french jazz
rag: "Petit Walter est Mort"

Walter, you better watch yourself,
look at your shredded face:
solos too close to the sun
like your knife fights:
about passion, longing, scar tissue.
you whisper Juke, Juko, Jukare
into a mad dog's ear,
and
when you play, we stop breathing,
Walter,
you are dangerous.

III

(It's always nine below zero at 3 o'clock in the afternoon)

So each day, at noon, Sonny Boy used to hit the airwaves over
Arkansas; he sucked his desperate lyric from a harp shell like
he was taking Communion. The hoarse whisper of a man
hurting from profound thirst. Sonny Boy II was Shaky Tim's
favorite but Sonny was not the best choice to save him or to
invite introspection. Still, Tim couldn't lie to himself when
he broke into "Help Me" or ran through the outtakes and
forbidden passages of "Little Village." There is no room for
lying in those tunes. Otherwise, if Tim went into a confession
box, he'd have to pack a lunch. So, he never went there. He
rolled through the ambiguous teachings of his broken brother
and his wine soaked Dad, both preachers. He wasn't with
the church; he found his comfort in Sonny Boy. He learned
to work the harmonica, make it growl in the lower registers
so there was an edge to it. If you read Dante, you know that
where you lose the thread that's where you make your bed
and Tim lost it somewhere in the 13th Canto; when he went
down, he went down hard and he stayed down like a root
ball. He died in the bathroom, on cool tile, in a space that
barely held his fallen frame. He was dead before he hit the
floor. The report said "heart failure" but that was a metaphor
and everybody but Shaky's mom knew exactly what it meant.
Shaky Tim is buried 6 feet beneath the cliffs at Carpenteria
with a C harp at his chest. The wind is almost finished
forgetting about him; it's the wind has the last word.

a rendering

Bucks County,
late summer, 1963,
a rural crossroad.
The sultry heat
drops down,
starts to take over
from the cool of predawn.
A car slows for me,
my ride to the plant.
Then we are changing
into our greens,
our steel-toed boots,
descending
those waffled metal stairs
to the floor.

The trucks,
up from Delaware
with a cargo
of feather and bone,
are off-loaded into the pit.
(One rooster
made the whole trip
clinging to an axle.
A miracle. I took him home,
watched with admiration
as he wore the tail feathers
off all five of our hens.
We named him King Peter;
he lives in legend.)

It's 6 a.m. again
We receive the shovels
that never rest.
The handles damp and warm

from the graveyard shift.
Fire cookers the size of tankers
churn the once living parts.
Another steams blood,
turns it to powder.
When the cookers are ready,
they spit their issue
into the pit.
Grease drains below
through grated steel trays:
soap and lipstick
for the boulevard shops.
The hard stuff is shoveled
into a moving screw,
is carried back upstairs:
kibble for the pets,
even now dozing
at the foot
of a well made bed.
We bend over the trough,
raking and shoveling,
packaging in burlap
powdered blood
that holds our sweat,
turns to paste,
cakes in our hair.
We bend into the work,
feel sweat in our pits,
and cracks.
Pain stabs
into the small of the back.
We learn to breathe
without noticing the stench
that inhabits every pore
every cross-stitch.

We take salt pills
so we don't pass out
in the dizzy heat.

I decide to learn harmonica,
to learn the work songs,
to play "I've Been Doin'
Some Hard Travelin'."
I want to play
what it's all about,
learn to play
while the screw,
steady grinding, moves, twists,
yet stays in one place.
I need to make
a sound track,
ordinary chords
for 6 a.m.
when the hard travelin'
really begins.

Recovery

I crave the orange,
the sugar
might bring me back to life,
a fierce revisitation
in slow motion
so I can study the game film.
I devour the orange
ripping at pulp,
salvaging any episodic lucidity.
I have too much to learn
at the blackboard
in a fast falling dusk.
If you lie in a hospital bed
cranked into position
there is fluorescent light,
neat porous squares of
acoustical ceiling tile,
the curved track of the modesty curtain.
Here, there is no private dying.
Every stirring clears that linen barrier.
Final shakings and rattlings find ways.
In some distant tree,
the jarring squawk of blue jays
rings with hope.
I'm like a rootball
seeking shoots, tendrils or
any sprinkling of real light.
I travel where underbrush is expectant.
The poems, when they come,
cover what came before
and they shine before they are covered themselves.
Rotation of crops fuels innocence,
makes topsoil black with promise.

They say that once I understand
that certain things whispered in the background
give power, I could reach a new plateau.
I listen: carts on wheels, soap operas
and storm warnings, the way
nursing shoes squeak and I listen
past these dense cinder blocks, to
traffic, to the racket of the jays
and to the very breath
of this building: refrigeration,
the modal hum of air conduction,
until I am still and breathless.
I see terra cotta
holding aloe vera and chamomile.
There is sun on the veranda,
my wife is making bread
and morning is all I know.

The Dentist's Chair

My tongue
is a mangled war machine.
The dentist asks me,
"is there some kind
of systemic disease process?"

I don't know. Maybe
the blues has taken its toll.
Or just rage, debate
and other mad curvatures.

In the dentist's chair,
the tongue is still and silent,
not at peace,
just tucked out of
harm's way.

Better Than Memory

To close my eyes tight
and still see a window:
black on red
all lines and panels intact;
the impression,
better than memory,
taps me on the shoulder
for a time,
it's an afterburner,
a red and vivid scarring
of retinal tissue
and better than memory,
it melts away,
never stings or disfigures:
water strokes on hot pavement.

The sound of the ceiling fan
the soft voices
of Erika and Wendy in the kitchen
over cigarettes and ice creme bars
at midnight,
probably a perfect moment.

When you close your eyes
all the lines are there
holding it together.

The impression,
better than memory.

distance*

Tracks slice through Belgium
without me.
Nearing Paris:
communication wire,
imperfect parallels,
the same sun,
cows leaning against posts, etc.

I'm 80 miles east of Needles now,
aimed at the mountains,
thinking of thunder
and the backs of your knees;
thinking of you
unrolling your dark stockings
while Hurricane Belle
beats Long Island to death.

Mariachi music moves across the desert
like locusts.
Spanish newscasts swarm around my ears.
The radio &
the wind;
it's the only way to stay awake.
Tracks hum alongside me,
tracks tracing curvature,
tracks gathering first heat.

*for m.t. with respect to Reverdy

A Necklace Made of Water

She pictures how the river will shine
through a Pullman window.
It will be a necklace sparkling
in late afternoon.
She has planned the voyage carefully
and built in the usual drawbacks.
So she forgets certain things
to make it more likely
she will miss her train.
After all,
the voyage is the very absence
of the familiar.
So what does it matter
what she forgets?
She is willing,
time and time again,
to watch trains depart
without her.

There is a word for all this
but to say it
would make no sense.

Forgetting is her right.
It is.
And not bothering to pack
is her right.

Her hands hang at her sides,
gripping and releasing
as though they might
possess something.

The very absence.

hands that hold
(for Jean Valentine)

again the chaos
kettle drum prestissimo
blows my chest apart

against a wall
that yields
to the pounding

and becomes something
more than the eye or ear
can manage

submerges me
in the sweet foam
of an ancient river

if i can breathe
and rise to another surface
a surface of light

where notes blend
and hang on rhythm
i could find myself

crossing a white bridge
to hands that hold me
lead me

a path that can only
be seen in
the dark

Turning
(for Czeslaw Milosz)

If morning comes again,
I'll say, "Of course."
But the truth is,
in the pocket that is night,
dawn seems miraculous,
not a sure thing
at all.
In a stormy crease,
dinged by random change,
ricochets, large
and small,
I reach full gallop. For me,
movement is necessary,
tumbling toward something,
the shore, the promise of undercurrent,
open space, meteor showers.
Counting change is mixing metaphors,
stealing moments, stealing centimes, stealing
lines,
it puts me
up against myself.
Change, silver, like thunder where
light precedes sound but
no light can be seen
from in here.

What I know:
we're on a rock,
we spin through black space,
and make the best of it.

Signals
(after Jean Valentine)

A radio broadcast
a long time before me
but now I run to a place
where I can hear it clearly,
my father's studio,
dominated by the etching press
from the Chicago Art Institute.
It transmits, moist,
and squeezes out truth
like the secret signal
of nostrils,
nose to nose,
in the pasture
the way
we greet
a horse-
a strong signal,
an old signal.

But none of that matters now.
Everything breaks up
and comes apart.
I try to be what is needed,
to be what I can. To be

the wind.
That other wind.
The one that lifts the bandana.
Colors,
ragged on a barbed wire fence
in the north
of New Mexico.

Like streams.

Rorschach

Two Haitians are cooking something in a pot,
 I don't venture a guess.
Amoebas or continents
divide. What's next?
Moths and shellfish,
thunderheads, pelvic rotations
inky and grey.
When I see the eighth card,
red and grainy,
I come unglued.
Clinical signs begin spilling
all over my lap
with a snot like irreverence
for identifiable shape.
My windpipe stops working,
my eyes twitch. Feet
and hands
go their separate ways. I say,
"Sometimes a vagina is
just a vagina."
They could lock me down for this
or they might let me
talk for hours,
just to see what else I know.
Poet or madman,
do we make a choice?
When I take pumice
to my inky fingers,
classic scenes come to mind.

These cards,
like unsorted snapshots,
so neat in a pile,
unwind me, spin me,
compel me to talk
to people whose language
I don't recognize.

I long for people
I've seen for the last time.

vanishing point

you are chased by a gang
it is after your anger
the enemy is on foot
and your fear recedes

then you are on a beach
recognition alone burning
an enemy ship spots you walking
angles into your foreground

you prepare a list of natural disasters
you have located a vanishing point
and pretend to light a panatella
where the tracks converge

you are chased by a gang
the enemy is on foot
then you are on a beach
an enemy ship spots you walking

you prepare a list of natural disasters
and pretend to light a panatella

it is after your anger
and your fear recedes
recognition alone burning
angles into your foreground

you have located a vanishing point
where the tracks converge

pebble game
(after Cendrars and The Parker Brothers)

the child's sucker
is a moon on a stick

a broken globe
flung into a southerly
orbit

a pretense of rain
the dice tumbling
across the board
in their time

a silver gun ship
that won't float

a silver dog
the bark in progress

a top hat
a boot a
steam iron
you know the rest

the thimble protects
a girl's finger tip from
any careless prick

we have a red hotel,
hollow;
expensive shoes in the hall

an unfolding white square
the children crowding in
blowing their gold

a rosy fist perforates the magnetic dawn.
it streaks across yellow sky, rolls through
pockets of radio signals in an ancient arc
to destroy a toy gone awry

after blowing down The Arc De Triomphe
the children toss off a laugh
that shatters windows in Berlin.
we are snacks for their crazy teeth

we are underground now a
good eye is glued
to what is said to be
a star
a rock painted
on a rock

everybody says it's been raining
steadily
listen
bored little fingers
trot the boardwalk

I am a blurry
horse on fire
in the hills it
hasn't rained for months

They are approaching The Bench tossing sacred robes
and documents into space like words of praise. A guard
picks up a stool. The brittle eyes of Mother Justice spill
out of her stone head and roll down the marble steps
like lonely planets. One bounces off an empty dog. We
crouch at the mouth of July and listen for the sound.
We are victims of rolling blackouts and strange ricochets.

When My Ride Shows

Big homes
have outlying territories,
other bedrooms
where you can get lost
in pretense.

Little apartments
have tiny yellow tables
for toast and promises.

The narrow path,
the shallow creek
small talk
enough to fill the room.
And then the heart
with all its treacherous circuitry.

The space between us
fills with heat,
with a sudden interest
in Latin percussion.

I've lost the words
for ending sentences
but when my ride shows,
none of that will matter.

In white light,
when fever
is the only truth,
a question will occur
and the answer
will explain
almost everything.

Layover

a letter from Iceland
I didn't notice the stamp
I'll bet it was a snow scene
icebergs and freighters
with some odd value affixed
in the corner
next to something
looking like a music staff
and the letter itself
I did notice that
it was from you
you devil
changing planes no doubt
off to Belgium
just to listen
to the cabs and ambulances
roll by
blowing horns and sirens
going flat
by degrees

How It Leads To The Next

No one passes soundlessly,
not in this life.

I recognize the sound
of your hair being brushed,
your blood spinning
over at the lab,
the rustle of nylons
where your legs come together;
that's when wisdom falls away
like a rock slide.

You remind us we ache for home,
you remind us
we are shaped by heat and brick,
carved by hope.

Every man must carry his sleepy child
out under the night sky
to count stars and planets
out loud
to remember there is a vast heaven
swimming in those wide
and tiny globes.

Death Bed Blues

"Heaven for the climate,
Hell for the company"
       —Mark Twain

Let the near silence
do its work.
It's always in the present tense.
Maybe in the swell of a heartless wind,
the whisper of nylons crossed high,
the brush of folding money
sliding into an empty pocket.
Even the final breath of the old man
alone in a riverfront hotel,
a small room
in a small town he's never seen.
Where blue light
spells HOT-L
outside the window.

He's remembering, as a kid
staying awake until 3 a.m.,
afraid he'd stop breathing.
Those nights whispered in rhythm,
in and out of rhythm.
He'd wait for the fear
to disappear.

Is this his season in Hell
or does that come next?
On his bed,
under a broken ceiling fan,
he can smile,
expecting,
sometime in the
present tense,
at least good company
and a warm beer.

We'll All Go Together

I'm there on a barstool
knocking them back
cold and in bottles
watching my reflection,
wondering how I'll go.

By thirst or hunger
ear splitting glass filled thunder
out on the East River Drive.
A slow silent growth
inside the chest,
an inferno over Kansas,
high in an otherwise untroubled sky.
Or a bullet to the head
when I walk into some mini-mart
in San Bernardino
for a damn Mars bar.

Or what if I trade it all
for something that shines,
something held up in the distance,
a gold certificate,
something wrapped in silver foil.

Later,
I walk a dirty sidewalk
where spit shines like diamonds
where neon lights the way.

I'm thinking,
we'll all go together,
it'll be over
in a moment.

DETAIL OF A PRINT OUT

```
27035Go To 174
30000SUBROUTINE RETALIATION
30005U=(AND(2) * PC) * 1
30010D=A*D
30015C=INT(6)
30017S=S+D
30020IF  S>=100   GO TB  30100
30025RETURN
30100FOR Z = 1 TH *
30105SUBROUTINE RETALIATION
30110NEXT Z
```

```
30121 TAB(10);   BBBBBB        NNN    NNN       AA              GGGG
30122 TAB(10);   BBBBBBB       NNN    NNN       AAA            GGGGGG
30123 TAB(10);   BBBBBBBB      NNN NNN NNN      AAAAAA         GGGGGGG
30124 TAB(10);   BBB    BBB    NNNNNN NNN       AAAAAA        GGGG  GGG
30125 TAB(10);   BBB    BBBB   NNNNNNN NNN      AAA   AAA     GGG    GG
30126 TAB(10);   BBB    BBBB   NNNNNNNNNNN      AAA   AAA     GGG
30127 TAB(10);   BBBBBBBB      NNNNNNNNNNN      AAA   AAA     GGG   GGGGGG
30128 TAB(10);   BBBBBBBB      NNNNNNNNNNN      AAAAAAAAA     GGG   GGGGGG
30129 TAB(10);   BBBBBBBBBB    NNNNNNNNNNN      AAAAAAAAA     GGG     GG
30130 TAB(10);   BBB    BBBB   NNNNNNNNNNN      AAAAAAAAA     GGG     GG
30131 TAB(10);   BBB    BBB    NNNNNNNNNNN      AAA   AAA     GGG     GG
30132 TAB(10);   BBB    BBBB   NNN    NNNN      AAA   AAA     GGGG   GGG
30133 TAB(10);   BBBBBBBBBB    NNN    NNN       AAA   AAA     GGGGGGGG
30135 TAB(10);   BBBBBBB       NNN    NNN       AAA   AAA      GGGG
30140 FOR Z=1 TO 3
30145 NOTHING YET
30150 NEXT Z
30156 WHEN THROUGH, SIGN OFF BY INPUTING>OFF<
30160 INPUT OFF
30165 GO TO 99900
40000 NEW POSITION SUBROUTINE
40005 O3=(RNU(2)=RO)+1
40010 O3=INT (O3) NOTHING YET
```

The Devil's Advice To Virginia Woolf

Here is the well
that has sustained you.
Roses and mulberries
have taken over
but the well is deep
and the water is cold.

Chilly chemistry
and a busy undercurrent
lick at surfaces.

Good water
bad water,
it's all the same for dying.

Put stones and pennies
in your apron;
they will help you locate
solitude and depth.

On Main Street

On Main Street
in some jerkwater town
just past the Platte River
where the wild west really begins,
where the wind
walks upright
and pounds its chest,
where there's nothing to stop it
but silent mountains
400 miles away,
a woman stares out her window.

Something in her eyes
comes unhooked.
The dark is coming
and closing fast.

What she sees
is dust, dry heat
and a hopeless horizon.
She's coming to terms
with truth.
She's always known
it's hers to ignore.
She's always known
why she lies.
She can't forget the truth,
but she'd like to
and if she could,
maybe these lies
would become her truth,
her miracle.
To lie you must believe.

She stubs out her cigarette,
bites at her lip,
steps back from the window,
her history bursting open,
spilling what she's lost.

She's no longer on the outskirts
of losing control,
she's on Main Street.

And without an angel.

She can tear you apart
with a kiss of indifference.
It's the best
you can hope for.

Small Talk
(after Gregory Corso)

I tried to warn him
but he wouldn't listen
I told him, "rage,
let it sleep.
It will burst into wakefulness
when the time arises."
He threw back another
and said,
"endure the night
feel the impact of the heat;
it'll come down off the top rope,
knees first.
Eventually, we're all
just a cross
out by the highway."
Then he laughed and said,
"you know, sometimes
I can see clear through
to the other side."
That's when I knew it was on.
He continued,
"down in the islands
where the voodoo and the saints come from,
there's no gravity to worry about anyway.
The river speaks,
the rock spins,
we come, we go.
The flat grey stone
skips the surface
with momentary flair."

I was trying to figure out
how that all fit
so I said,
"Oh yeah, are we just accidents,
some kind of bumper car
pile up at Coney Island?
Just take your time
getting to the point
cause I'm going to live forever."

I could feel myself
slipping toward the low ground,
toward that episodic lucidity
where shallow
is as deep as it gets.

I was still drinking Cuervo Gold back then
and I ordered another.
He said, "you boil a pigeon's ass
and it tastes better than that shit."

I can't let any of that bother me though.
Besides, he might be right.
There may be pearls
in the mouth of the dragon.
You never know
when you'll meet your match.

In the end
it's all small talk.

And a helluva lot of it.

buses

a black woman
on a bus bench
waiting in silence
lost in something
that waiting does

a black woman
a lime green blouse
limp on her chest from
heat and from the waiting

(some buses appear to slow
and tempt her with boarding
but they are
buses unable
to stop moving
buses ripe
with possibilities
of destination
with timetables
and dance cards
of their own)

sudden acceleration
leaves her standing
leaves her
learning
to be
still

Certainty

In the late hours,
where the once gaping mouth
of the future
closes by the minute,
she lights a cigarette,
heads for home.
She knows
there's not much time on the clock.
She finds her street.
She finds her key.
There is cognac
and a warm bed inside.
That is enough.

But just to be sure
she pats herself twice
at the heart,
turns the key.

Just to be sure.

Judy In Santa Fe

You're selling Navajo rugs
to a deaf lady
down on The Square.
She needs your lips,
she steps toward you,
parts your hair like a curtain
to see your lips.
You are talking about the red dye,
how they make it
from a thousand crushed beetles.
She needs your lips
to know
how they make red.

White Kitchen
(toward a line by Laurel Ann Bogen)

Your taste was never that princely.
It had origins in some border town.
How did so many fish heads end up down there?
The Rio Grande is supposed to be dry, man.
Bad weather & bad tuna.
It seems funny now
after 30 years.
I knew I was breathing too hard
in that huge white kitchen
at that yellow table
when you resisted
the temptation to plunge
a steak knife into my chest.
When I'm honest with myself
I admit it was one of those times
when being speechless
would have helped.

Never silent,
the white kitchen,
a riot of sound.
Amidst tomatoes
and other perfect fruit,
we painted it.
There were other rooms
to hide in.

So, we broke a few plates
in that white kitchen.
It's true.
We were crazy,
crazy with hope.

Erika Spray Paints Till Dawn

Late July and the night
moves restless. Under the
bright moon, 6 coyotes
and a Union Pacific freight
carry on in milky light.
I lie in bed, one hand at my heart,
the other on private equipment.
It's a good sign. It means
I might live.

You say, "It's a good night to
spray paint some furniture."

I think when both hands are at the heart
they may have been placed there
by a third party.
I've never trusted that.
It's better when elements
line up and circumstances
lend themselves. We know
there is a right time,
a perfect time,
and tonight, in this pale
rustling light, spray paint
in turquoise
and never forget.

Let no distance obscure
this turquoise.
In my mind
there is you
pressing a little red button
and making turquoise
in the night. And
in a noisy July dawn
a storage cabinet
glows turquoise
glows quiet.

At Santa Monica and Western

You're been touched up
and your game's gone south.
Now you're just a battered pitcher
in black relief
against the sun blanched corner
at Santa Monica and Western.

A long red light
compels us to watch your windup.
You pull at your cap,
pound your glove,
check the runners,
shake off signs
and whisper the count
with lips that never stop moving.

You arm wrestle with the wind,
quite delirious with your stuff
and you wait for the medicine to work.
Just like the rest of us.

Medicine Fields

The medicine fields surround us,
smother us with hope.
We sacrifice reason
by degree
until heat and dread stack up
like boxes in a warehouse.
You are here with me,
begging for deliverance.

Our old dog
claws at moonlight,
scratches at Mexican tile,
a crackling fire
in her little death dream.

Mexican Blue *(for Ruby)*

She speaks
through configuration.
An arrangement of cards
on a table, broken tile
and mexican blue shards,
laid out in rune,
in cipher. She
is talking about the movies again.
In an early Egypt life,
she died young
but learned to speak
without words.

Now, she offers pieces of pottery
from indian digs in Broken Arrow
and Tuba City. She's landed
without identification. There is only
a hastily acquired visitor's visa,
an afterthought really (and
this amuses her).
She's not from here
but she likes the movies.
She watches with the sound turned off
and she's the first
to admit it.

From his lips, Erika

There is no mental flexibility
where axons curl
and hang like sheared chain-link,
tweaked and sprung,
stretched beyond repair.
A synapse
like a footbridge
crossing neuro-vascular rubble,
no longer secure
in north light,
leads to the wrong bingo parlor
where everybody smokes
and nobody wins.
We enter problematic space
causing electrical storm
hemispheric collision
unpedigreed disarray.

You say,
"My name is what you breathe,
Air-i-ka." And
that's how people remember you.
People with bad memories,
people with brain damage
and no future,
people who can't remember
their lunch
remember you
and that's how they do it,
your name,
it's what they need,
it's what they breathe.

Even old man Lester,
he shot himself in the head
but he missed so bad
he has to go around
in a wheelchair
hitting everybody with a stick.

You pick flowers
and he
lets you
put them
in his hand.

Real Poetry

I was still a kid.
It was late November on Route 413,
Pineville, Pennsylvania.
The ghosts were restless
on the porch of the general store,
the only store in town.
In the distance,
the sound of a hammer
ringing off cold steel,
pounding lonesome at dusk.
My Dad says, "son,
that's real poetry
right there."

Years after,
on the day we buried my Dad,
me and Bernie
raised a couple cold Rolling Rocks
at The Pineville Tavern,
the only bar in town.
We clicked those long necks
and talked about Dad.
He was with us for a moment.
There was motion, I swear
in that smoky tavern air.

Some guy down the bar
started mad-doggin' me.

Real poetry,
right there.

Also by Rick Smith

PRODUCER *(with John Lyon)*

Steve Mann Live At The Ash Grove (Half Blind's Choice, 1975; lp)
and (Bella Roma Music, 2008; cd)

ANTHOLOGIES

Foreign Exchange, a clack of American poets (Biographics, 1979)
The Aspect 10 Year Anthology (Zephyr Press, 1981)
Eyes Like Mingus (LUMMOX Press, 1999)
Lost Highway (LUMMOX Press, 2002)
So Luminous The Wildflowers (Tebot Bach, 2003)
Familiar (The People's Press, 2005)
Hunger Enough (Puddinghouse Publications, 2005)
a chaos of angels (Word Walker, 2006)
The Best of Little Red Books (LUMMOX Press, 2009)
The Long Way Home (LUMMOX Press, 2009)
Reeds and Rushes (Puddinghouse Publications, 2010)
Last Call: The Bukowski Legacy Continues
        (LUMMOX Press, 2011)
Working The Wreckage of the American Poem
        (LUMMOX Press, 2011)
Cradle Songs (Quill & Parchment Press, 2012)
Impact: An Anthology of Short Memoirs
        (Telling Our Stories Press, 2012)
Cartography (Imagination and Place Press, 2013)
Summer Anthology (Silver Birch Press, 2013)
Together Again For The First Time (Parks, 2013)

Bernie Van Leer

RICK SMITH GREW UP on the lower East Side of NYC before the family moved to Bucks County, Pa. There was also a year or so in Paris. The writing began in high school, poems inspired by William Blake and Carl Sandburg. His English teacher at Solebury School was Michael Casey who would include Yeats, William Burroughs and rock writers Leiber and Stoller in the same lesson plan. Smith went on to study with Anthony Hecht at Bard College where Hart Crane's "The Bridge" made a big impact. At the same time, music began to take an important role. With no formal training (one lesson from Chevy Chase, one from James Cotton), Smith learned blues harmonica and went to work on the streets of Greenwich Village, playing for tips or meals, rubbing shoulders with youngsters like Cass Elliott, Bob Dylan, Richie Havens, Steve Stills and the guys in The Lovin' Spoonful. Dylan actually had to borrow Smith's harmonica for an impromptu set at Bard one night. He delivered a car to California in 1965 and founded The City Lights late that year. He starved on the Sunset Strip, selling candy door to door by day, playing for a piece of the door or for free at clubs like the Sea Witch, The Galaxy, Bido Lito's and The Whiskey. The band played those infamous Be-In concerts at Griffith Park and actually opened for

Smokey Robinson and The Miracles at the Cheetah in Venice Beach, in 1967.

In the mid 1970s, Smith joined Dan Ilves to co-edit the literary journal Stonecloud. His interview with Tom Waits in issue #7 made it a sought after collector's item. In 1976, he played on the soundtrack of the Oscar-nominated film, "Days of Heaven." In 1981, he and collaborator John Lyon wrote and recorded "Hand To Mouth," a well-reviewed LP of originals which got substantial air-play. He went on to write and record with Mindless, Go Figure, The Hangan Brothers and The Mescal Sheiks. Smith continues to perform, write and record with The Sheiks and with Music Formula; new releases from both bands are in the works. Poems have appeared widely in journals like New Letters, The Wormwood Review, South Bay Magazine, Rattle and Spillway...

A string of day jobs evolved, unpredictably, to a late career as a clinical psychologist. He spent several years on the internationally acclaimed neurology service at Rancho Los Amigos Medical Center. He is now in private practice in Rancho Cucamonga, CA where he lives with his wife and son.

ABOUT THE LUMMOX PRESS

LUMMOX Press was created in 1994 by **RD Armstrong**. It began as a self-publishing/DIY imprint for poetry by RD, aka Raindog. Several chapbooks were published and in late 1995 LUMMOX began publishing the *LUMMOX Journal,* a monthly small/underground press lit-arts mag. Available primarily by subscription, the *LJ* continued its exploration of the "creative process" until its demise as a print mag in 2006. It was hailed as one of the best monthlies in the small press by John Berbrich and Todd Moore.

In 1998, LUMMOX began publishing the Little Red Book series, and continues to do so, sporadically, today. To date there are some 60 titles in the series and a collection of poems from the first decade of the series has been published under the title **The Long Way Home** (2009); it's a great way to explore the series.

Together with Chris Yeseta (Layout and Art Direction since 1997), RD continues to publish books that are both striking in their looks as well as their content…*published because of the merit of the work, not the fame of the author.* That's why there are so many first full-length collections in the roster (look for the *****).

*   *   *

The following books are available directly from the LUMMOX Press via its website: ***www.lummoxpress.com*** or at LUMMOX c/o PO Box 5301 San Pedro, CA 90733. There are also E-Copy (PDF) versions of most titles available. Books with the letters SPD are also carried by Small Press Distribution.

The Wren Notebook by Rick Smith (2000)
Last Call: The Legacy of Charles Bukowski
   edited by RD Armstrong (2004)
On/Off the Beaten Path by RD Armstrong (2008)
Fire and Rain–Selected Poems 1993-2007 Vols. 1 & 2 by
   RD Armstrong (2008)*

El Pagano and Other Twisted Tales by RD Armstrong
  (short stories – 2008)*
New and Selected Poems by John Yamrus (2009)
The Riddle of the Wooden Gun by Todd Moore (2009)
Sea Trails by Pris Campbell (2009)
**Down This Crooked Road–Modern Poetry from the
  Road Less Traveled** edited by RD Armstrong and William
  Taylor, Jr. (2009)
Drive By by John Bennett (2010)
Modest Aspirations by Gerald Locklin & Beth Wilson
  (2010)
Steel Valley by Michael Adams (2010)*
Hard Landing by Rick Smith (2010)
A Love Letter to Darwin by Jane Crown (2010)*
E/OR—Living Amongst the Mangled
  by RD Armstrong (2010)
Ginger, Lily & Sweet Fire by H. Lamar Thomas (2010)*
Whose Cries Are Not Music by Linda Benninghoff (2011)*
Dog Whistle Politics by Michael Paul (2011)*
What Looks Like an Elephant by Edward Nudleman
  (2011)* SPD
Working the Wreckage of the American Poem
  edited by RD Armstrong (2011)
Living Among the Mangled (revised)
  by RD Armstrong, special edition, (2011)
The Accidental Navigator by Henry Denander (2011)
Catalina by Laurie Soriano (2011)* SPD
Born to Be Blue by Tony Moffeit (2011)
Last Call: the Bukowski Legacy Continues
  edited by RD Armstrong (2011)
Strong As Silk by Brigit Truex (2012)* SPD
The Instrument of Others by Leonard J. Cirino (2012)
If It We by Lisa Zaran (2012)*
The Names of Lost Things by Jason Hardung (2012)

Because, Just Because by Philip Ramp (2012)
Crazy Bone by Billy Jones (2012)
LUMMOX #1 edited by RD Armstrong (see description
  below)(2012)
5150–A Memoir by Dana Christensen (2013)*
I See Hunger's Children by normal (2013)*
her by j/j hastain (2013)*
How Long the Night Is by Christine DeSimone (2013)*
Songs of the Glue Machines by Nicolas Belardes (2013)
Breaking and Entering by D. R. Wagner (2013)
Me First by Ann Curran (2013)
What the Wind Says by Taylor Graham (2013)
Birth Mother Mercy by Alex Frankel (2013)*
Broken Lines–The Art & Craft of Poetry
  by Judith Skillman (2013)
LUMMOX #2 edited by RD Armstrong (2013)
Whispering in a Mad Dog's Ear by Rick Smith (2014)
Once You Start Eating, You Will Never Stop
  by Tim Peeler (2014)
Wildwood by Kyle Laws (2014)
Pleasure in a Stained Universe by Norman Olson (2014)*

* * *

LUMMOX (the anthology) returned in November of 2012
as a yearly print anthology. It contains interviews, essays, articles,
reviews, artwork, ads and lots of poetry (future issues will also
feature special flashbacks to the old *LUMMOX Journal* archives).
The focus of the first issue was "Favorite Poems," the theme for
#2 is PLACE. Each issue features poetry from around the world,
and is presented, in part, by "Guest Editors" (poets themselves)
who highlight some of their favorite poets.

LUMMOX is available by annual subscription for $25 USA
and $35 WORLD. Visit *www.lummoxpress.com/journal.html*
for details.

www.ingramcontent.com/pod-product-compliance
Lightning Source LLC
Chambersburg PA
CBHW020919090426
42736CB00008B/701